Revised Edition

Collins

Knowledge Lighthouse

A SKILL-BASED COURSE ON GENERAL KNOWLEDGE

1

Seema Chari
Kunal Savarkar

Components of DigiSuite

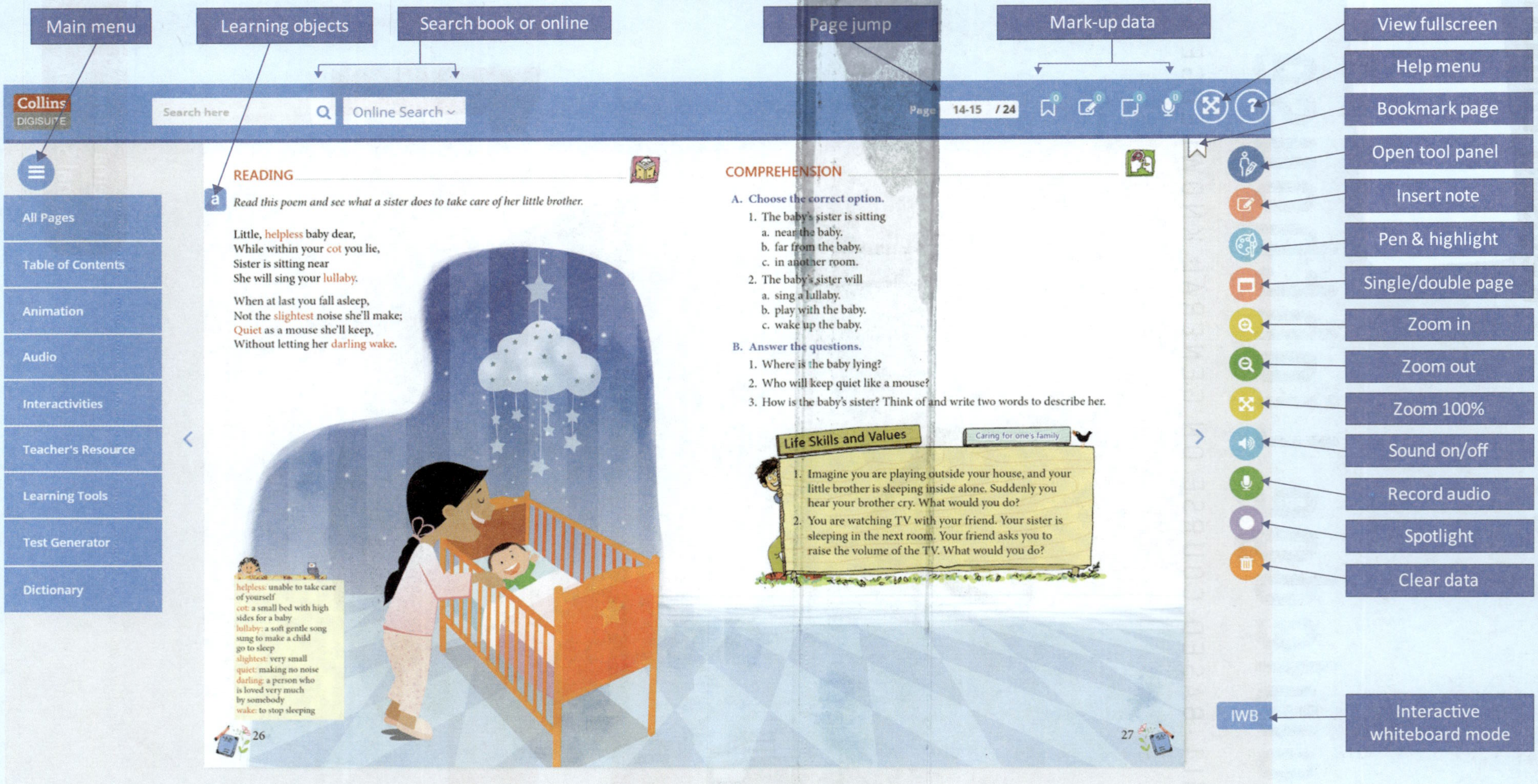

Student + Teacher

- **a** animations
- **ilt** instructor-led tutorials
- **ia** activities
- **w** worksheets
- **g** games
- **v** videos

Teacher-only

- **lp** lesson plans
- **w** worksheets
- **tn** teacher's notes
- **ak** answer keys

Preface

Like the universe, knowledge, too, is limitless. No matter how much we know, there is always more to know. In the 21st century, thanks to the leaps that technology has made and continues to make, we shall have to gather knowledge throughout our lives; so much so that we have coined a new portmanteau, to describe it: 'upskilling'.

Another novelty of the third millennium is how we access and absorb knowledge. Apart from human sources (family, teachers, friends), there are the online ones (website, social media). Yet, despite all this easy availability and accessibility, it is not always easy to distinguish between real and fake, relevant and redundant, significant and inconsequential.

Knowledge Lighthouse Revised Edition is a series meant for GenZ, that is, learners born after Y2K. The series covers 'classic' general knowledge content for learners of grades 1 to 8, but lays special emphasis on skills —learning skills, literacy skills and life skills— as well as knowledge gleaned from new learnings of the past few years, from COVID-19 to sustainability, from data science to global issues in an ever-shifting, ever-ephemeral, post-information world. All the new chapters, although dealing with topics of great gravity, are presented in an age-appropriate and friendly manner so as to kindle interest and lay the foundation for more in-depth learning.

A critical component of the Knowledge Lighthouse Revised Edition books is the India content, wherein our country in all its complexity and diversity is presented through colourful, simple and exciting tasks, plus brand-new features such as state-focus, city-focus and visit-a-monument.

A particularly career-friendly inclusion in the Knowledge Lighthouse Revised Edition series is Science, technology, engineering and mathematics (STEM), the disciplines of the future, and new global issues, presented under World Today. We hope to lighten these subjects for students, by adding a little sprinkle of trivia to them.

Sustainable development is one of the key phrases of this millennium, but what does it really mean for us, especially for children? The all-new Life on Land and Climate Action chapters not only sensitise learners but also encourage direct and immediate action.

In the Skills pages, the life skills section has tasks on safety and self-awareness. Connecting the dots is the foundation of knowledge and the series has chapters based on Higher Order Thinking Skills (HOTS) and critical thinking to train young minds to see patterns, learn to eliminate or choose details and observe better.

Become a Champion Quizzer

Knowledge Lighthouse Revised Edition encourages all learners to be curious and explore the world around them. Those who observe and absorb all the time, learn from everyone and everything; they are the ones who become quizzers. Here are six rules that will help you become a champion quizzer.

1. Be curious—look around you, see everything, read everything.
2. Listen to others.
3. Seek out new experiences.
4. Learn to link events and people.
5. Do your own research and learn to spot fake news.
6. Remember, no matter how much you know, there is much more that you have yet to learn.

Now, go for it! We are sure that this series will expose a whole new generation of learners to the fun universe of general knowledge and enhance their love for learning and discovery.

~ Seema Chari and Kunal Savarkar

In this series ...

Knowledge Lighthouse tasks are thematic and linear with visual, verbal, and strategic inputs to help students solve them and acquire knowledge through a wide range of subjects and themes.

World Around Us

18 Day Sky, Night Sky

We see different things in the sky in the day and at night. Look at the pictures and write D for things we see in the day and N for the things we see at night.

1 Butterfly 2 Stars 3 Sun 4 Bat

World Around Us tasks take the learners on an exciting journey across the world.

Natural World

3 Fruity Colours

In many fruits, the colour of the skin is different from the colour of flesh inside.

Look at the fruits and colour the inside part.

1 A watermelon is green ... outside

Natural World section uncovers the magical realm of plants, animals and birds.

Life on Land

9 Birthday Party for Planet Earth

Birthday parties are great fun. We meet our friends, dress up nicely, play games and eat yummy food. But so much gets wasted! From the decorations to the plates to treats, each party makes up a lot of trash. Let's plan a fun party without hurting our home, Planet Earth.

Here are some birthday party things. Some are good for the planet, some are not. Draw a 🙂 for the good things and a ☹ for the bad things.

Sustainable Development Goals sensitises learners towards sustainable development of the planet.

India Focus

26 We Celebrate

Look at the pictures of some festivals of India and write their names us... words given in the help box.

1 .... is the festival of lights.

India Focus tasks are created to evoke a sense of wonder and pride in our nation.

Art and Entertainment

13 Cartoon Characters

Mickey is a mouse and Donald is a duck.

Find out what these famous cartoon characters are and write the correct answers using the words given in the help box.

Art and Entertainment tasks celebrate artists, artworks, paintings, movies, awards and achievements.

Sports

21 Games We All Kno...

Using the words given in the help box, write the names of the games to which these terms belong.

1 Bowler Fielder Wicket

Sports section provides rules and records related to different sports.

Language and Literature

22 Taste Poem

Look at the pictures and complete this taste poem using the words given in the help box.

I like sweet things
Like ice cream and 1 ....
And pancakes with honey
And vanilla 2 ....!

Language and Literature tasks present vocabulary and etymology in a fun way.

World Today

29 Mask it up!

Read the following statements and choose the correct option.

1 We should/should not wear masks when we meet people, because of COVID.

Word Today introduces the learner to the COVID and post-COVID world.

Whiz fact

The national emblem of India has three lions standing on a band with a wheel at the centre. Below the wheel are the words *Satyameva Jayate*, which mean 'Truth Alone Triumphs'.

66

Whiz Fact is a spin-off fact about each topic or theme.

Whiz quiz

What is a scrap dealer called in your language?

Whiz Quiz are fun activities that encourage self-learning.

21st Century Skills

21st century skills are necessary to succeed in the Age of Information. These skills are divided into three main sets, namely, learning skills, literacy skills and life skills.

Learning Skills

- Critical Thinking and HOTS
- Creativity
- Collaboration
- Communication

Learning Skills

36 Stories of Fairies

Join the pictures and letters to write the names of some fairy tales.

1 Little + + Riding +

2 The + +

3 Snow + + and + the + 7 +

Literacy Skills

- Technology
- Information
- Media
- Financial Literacy
- Data Handling

Literacy Skills

42 Emoji Fun

Emojis are small pictures of faces, animals, people, common things and places. They are used to add feelings to messages sent through phones or computers.

Tick the correct emojis to match with the feelings.

1 Happy a b

2 Sleepy a b

3 Surprised a b

4 Bored a b

Life Skills

- Problem-solving
- Self-awareness
- Safety
- Social Skills

Life Skills

31 Safe at Home

Complete the sentences using words given in the help box.

1 If we walk with a glass full of water or milk, it can ....

2 If we open or close a door in a hurry, our finger can get ....

3 If we .... our fingers into electric sockets, we might get a shock.

Detailed Contents

Contents

1 This is Me

Complete this rhyme using the names of parts of the body given in the help box.

Chubby (1) ....

Dimpled (2) ....

Rosy (3) ....

(4) .... within

Curly (5) ....

(6) .... are brown,

Lovely and round

Mommy's pet, is that you?

Yes! Yes! Yes!

Sticking out (7) ....

One little (8) ....

Ten little (9) ....

Ten little (10) ....

(11) .... so clean

Smile so bright,

Lovely voice

Make some noise

Daddy's pet, is that you?

Yes! Yes! Yes!

Help box

fingers | chin | toes | Teeth | Eyes | ears | nose | lips | cheeks | Hands | hair

2 Good Morning

Tick (✓) the actions you do before going to school and cross (×) the actions you do not do before going to school.

1

Wake up ☐

2

Brush my teeth ☐

3

Tidy-out my closet ☐

4

Have a bath ☐

5

Put on party clothes ☐

6

Wear my socks and shoes ☐

7 

Eat breakfast

8 

Take off the uniform

9 

Go to the bus stop

10 

Take a long walk in the park

11 

Get on the school bus
after school

12 

Take a ride on a
merry-go-round

Whiz tip

A backpack is also called a rucksack. It is easier to carry a backpack if we wear the two straps on both shoulders.

3 Fruity Colours

In many fruits, the colour of the skin is different from the colour of the flesh inside.

Look at the fruits and colour the inside part.

1 A watermelon is green  outside

and red  inside.

2 A papaya is yellow  outside

and orange  inside.

3 A lychee is red  outside

and white  inside.

4 An apple is red  outside

and white 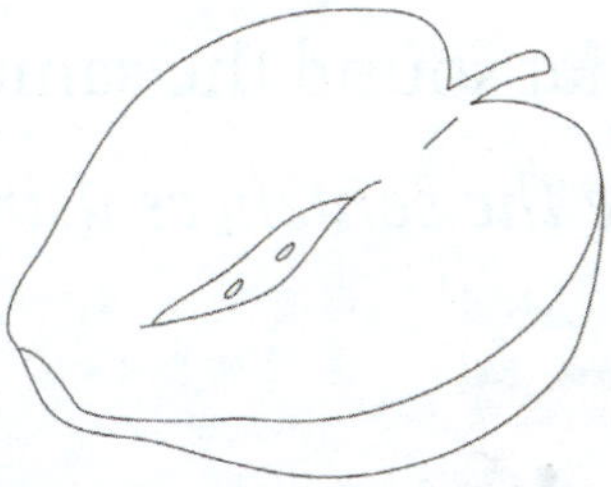 inside.

5 A mango is yellow  outside

and yellow 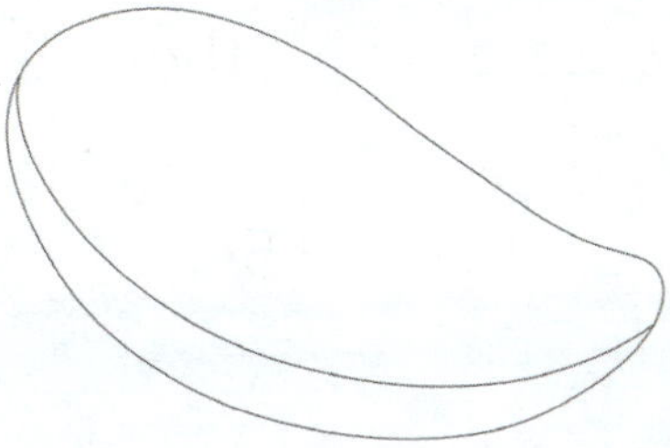 inside too.

6 A kiwi is brown  outside

and green 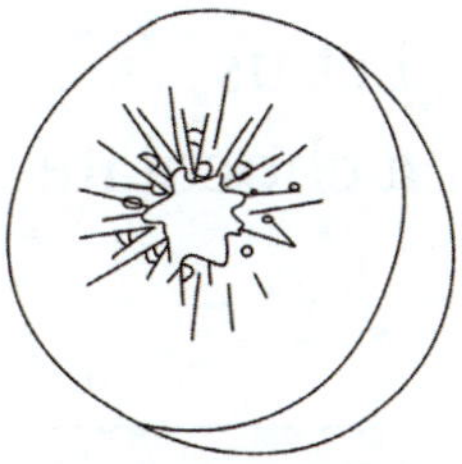 inside.

Whiz quiz

I have a green house
Inside that I have a brown house
Inside that I have a white house
Inside that I have a cupful of water.
What am I?

4 Easy-Peasy Words

Words that sound the same are called rhyming words.

Complete the sentences using the pairs of rhyming words given in the help box.

1 

The .... is on the ....

2 

The .... is on the ....

3 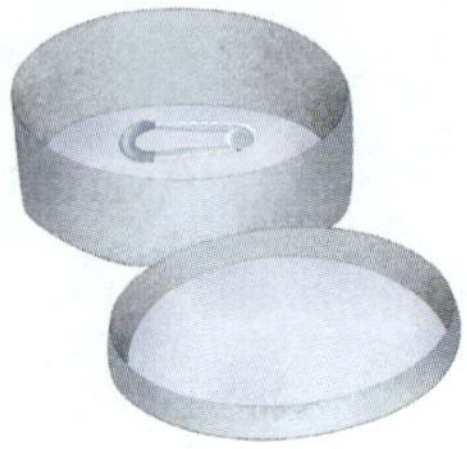

The .... is in the ....

4 

A .... and a ....

5 

Let us .... a chocolate ....

6 

The .... is in the ....

Help box

dog-log | bake-cake | cat-mat | jug-mug | pin-tin | mouse-house

Whiz quiz

Write two pairs of rhyming words.

1 ....

2 ....

Learning Skills

5 Happy Shapes

Look at these shapes and fill in the blanks with the names of colours given in the help box.

CRITICAL THINKING

1

The circle is ……………………………

2

The rectangle is ……………………………

3

The triangle is ……………………………

4

The diamond is ……………………………

5

The square is ……………………………

6

The star is ……………………………

Help box

yellow	orange	green	pink	purple	red

Whiz fact

A rectangle is like a square, but with two long sides and two short sides.

6 Animals and Birds

Have you visited a farm? A farm has many animals and birds. Look at these pictures and write A for animal and B for bird in the boxes given.

1 

Hen ☐

2 

Sheep ☐

3 

Duck ☐

4 

Horse ☐

5 

Cow ☐

6 

Rooster ☐

7 

Goose ☐

Whiz fact

Different farms have different names. Farms where fruits are grown are called orchards. Farms where tea and coffee are grown are called plantations.

7 I Can Do This

Tick (✓) the actions you can do yourself and cross (×) the actions you should not do on your own.

1

2

3

4

5

6

7

8

9

Whiz fact

Knives, scissors, paper-cutters and carpenter's tools are sharp objects. We should not use them on our own.

Sports

8 Let Us Play

Circle the things needed to play the given sport. One has been done for you.

1 Cricket

a 
Ball

b 
Bat

c 
Skate board

2 Football

a 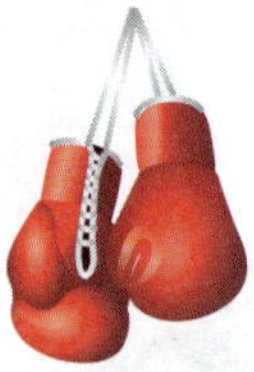
Gloves

b 
Cleats

c 
Ball

3 Table tennis

a 
Paddle

b 
Cue

c
Ball

4 Basketball

a 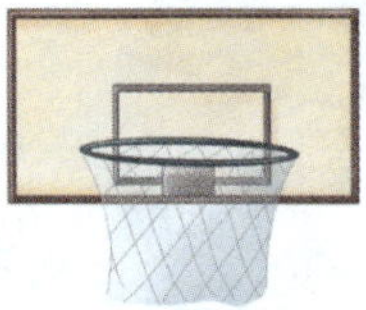
Basket

b 
Ball

c 
Wickets

5 Badminton

a 
Helmet

b 
Shuttlecock

c 
Racquet

Whiz fact

Golf balls were first made of wood, then of leather stuffed with goose feathers and now they are made of plastic and rubber.

15 LIFE ON LAND

Life on Land

9 Birthday Party for Planet Earth

Birthday parties are great fun. We meet our friends, dress up nicely, play games and eat yummy food. But so much gets wasted! From the decorations to the plates to treats, each party makes up a lot of trash. Let's plan a fun party without hurting our home, Planet Earth.

Here are some birthday party things. Some are good for the planet, some are not. Draw a 🙂 *for the good things and a* ☹️ *for the bad things.*

1 

Wrapping gift with newspaper

2 

Wrapping gift with a fresh brown paper

3 

Online invitation card

4 

Using brass plate and bowl

5 

Using cloth buntings

6 

Printed invitation cards

7 

Using plastic plates, cutlery and cups

8 

Giving a plant as a present

9 

Using Styrofoam

Whiz fact

Plastic straws take 200 years to break down and disappear. They are swallowed by animals, who choke on them and die. So don't drink out of plastic straws.

Literacy Skills

10 Big and Small Leaves

DATA HANDLING

Look at this picture with small and big leaves. Then read the lines. Are they correct or wrong?

Write ✓ in the box next to a correct line and × in the box next to a wrong line.

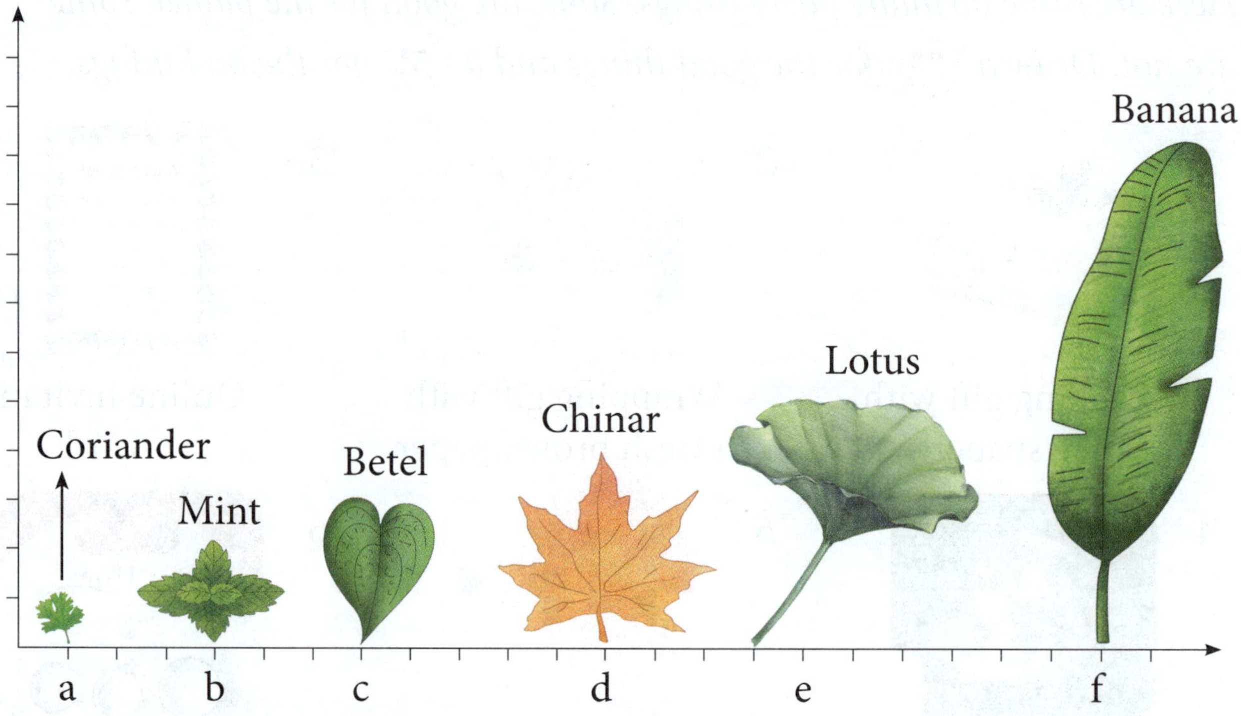

1 The coriander leaf is the smallest on this page. ☐

2 Lotus is the biggest leaf. ☐

3 Mint leaves are big but betel leaves are bigger. ☐

4 Chinar leaves and lotus leaves are the same size. ☐

5 Banana leaves are very big. ☐

Whiz quiz

The bayur tree is also called the dinner-plate tree because its leaves are round and huge. They can be used as real dinner plates.

Life Skills

11 Seeing with Our Hands

Imagine your eyes are covered with a scarf. What would these objects feel like when you touch them? Tick (✓) the correct words.

SELF AWARENESS

1

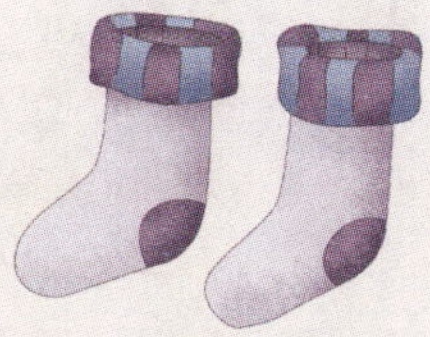

Socks

- [ ] Soft
- [ ] Hard

2

Candies

- [ ] Sticky
- [ ] Spongy

3

Apple

- [ ] Hard
- [ ] Rough

4

Eraser

- [ ] Pointy
- [ ] Spongy

5

Twig

- [ ] Rough
- [ ] Smooth

6

Pencils

- [ ] Pointy
- [ ] Round

Whiz fact

In Braille, letters are printed as groups of raised dots that we can feel with our fingers.

12 Food Animals Eat

Some animals are known to eat certain types of food.

Start at the red dot and trace over the wiggly lines to bring the animals to their food.

13 Cartoon Characters

Mickey is a mouse and Donald is a duck.

Find out what these famous cartoon characters are and write the correct answers using the words given in the help box.

1 

Minnie

....

2 

Scooby Doo

....

3 

Buzz

....

4 

Winnie-the-Pooh

....

5 

Simba

....

6 

Elsa

....

Help box

bear   mouse   lion   man   dog   girl

Whiz fact

The *Common Man* is a famous cartoon character made by the cartoonist RK Laxman. A statue of this cartoon character is in Pune.

14 The Right Place

Life Skills

Write the correct numbers of all these things inside their correct rooms.

1

Bucket

2

Ladle

3

Blanket

4

Pillow

5

Coffee table

6
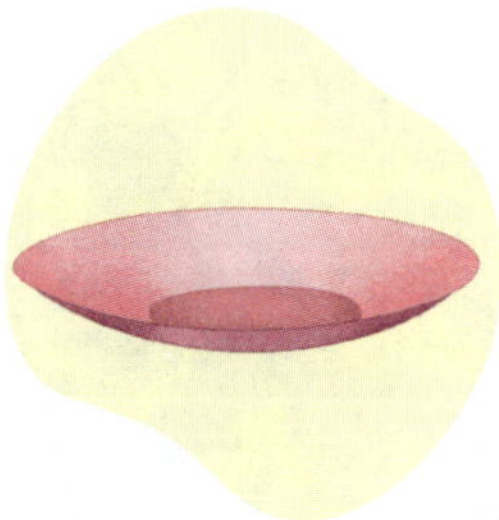
Plate

7

Car

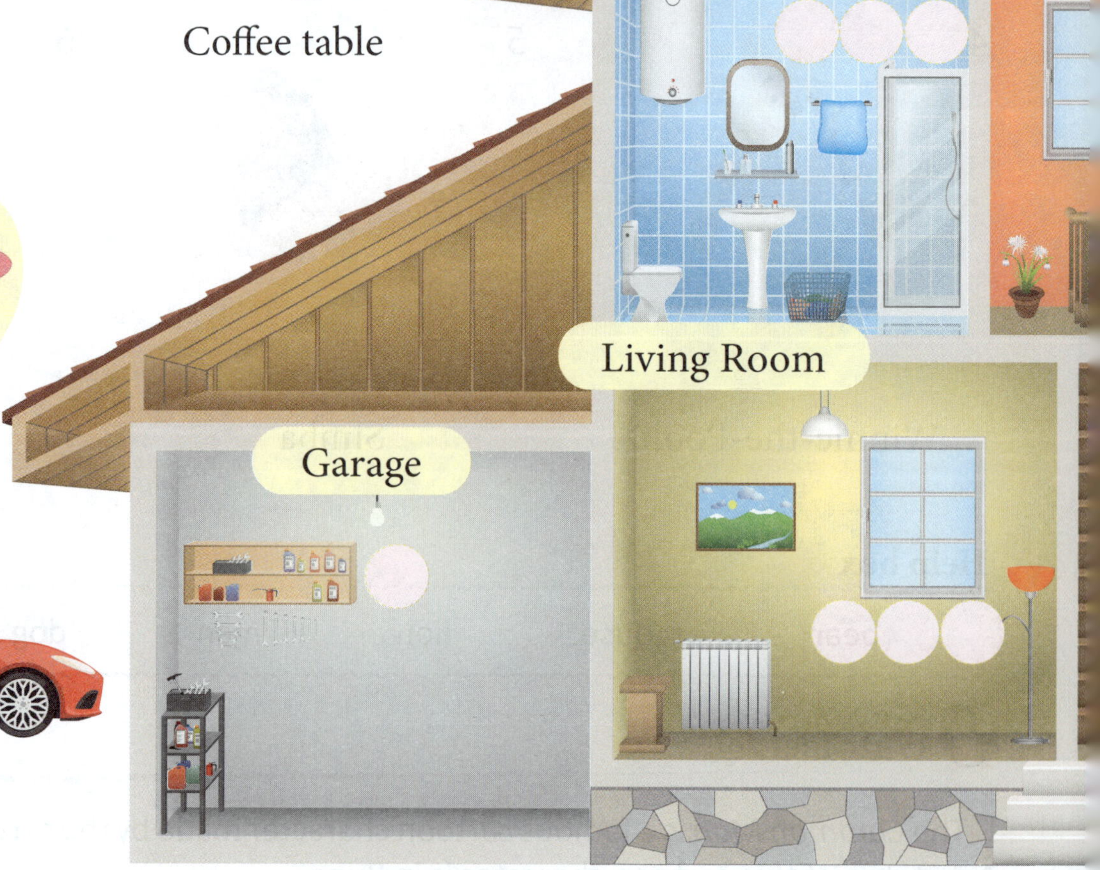

8

Bowl

9

Television

10

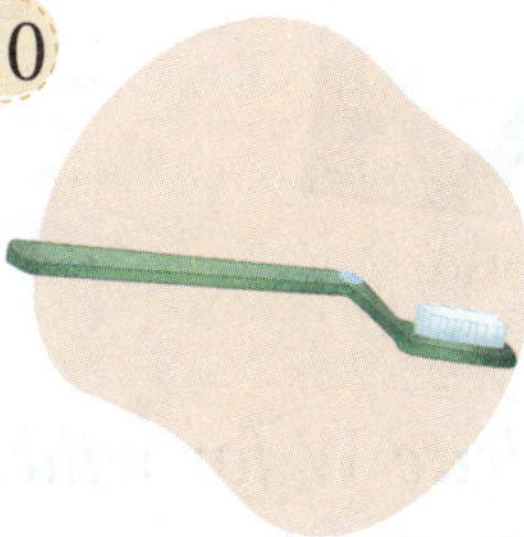

Toothbrush

11

12

Bed

13

Sofa

14

Soap

15

Clothes

15 Animals Around Us

Write W for wild animals and D for domestic animals.

1

Crocodile

2

Cat

3

Rhino

4

Lion

5

Dog

6

Tiger

7

Giraffe

8

Cow

9

Elephant

10

Goat

11

Bear

12

Horse

Whiz fact

The largest land animals are elephants, giraffes, rhinoceroses and hippopotamuses.

16 Action Words

Complete the poem with rhyming action words using the help box.

1 My pet dog loves to play
She loves to run and leap
But she just will not st ....
Oh, she makes me we ....!

2 She rips the couch at home
She .... ips Daddy all the time
She .... ps water from her dish
And Mommy's glass and mine.

3 She jumps and she licks
She .... mps
And she sticks
To me when I .... eep
Her love for me is so deep!

Help box

ay	si	tr	ep	sl	bu

Whiz fact

Words that are spelled almost the same might not rhyme. Think of good, food and flood!

Literacy Skills

17 Small to Big

DATA HANDLING

All living things grow. Write 1, 2 or 3 next to each living thing to arrange them from small to big. 1 stands for small, 2 stands for big and 3 stands for bigger.

A

Chick ☐

Egg ☐

Hen ☐

B

Tree ☐

Young plant ☐

Seed ☐

C

Eggs ☐

Frog ☐

Tadpole ☐

D

Girl ☐

Baby ☐

Woman ☐

Whiz fact

All living things need air, water and food to stay alive.

18 Day Sky, Night Sky

We see different things in the sky in the day and at night. Look at the pictures and write D for things we see in the day and N for the things we see at night.

1 Butterfly ☐

2 Stars ☐

3 Sun ☐

4 Bat ☐

5 Rainbow ☐

6 Moon ☐

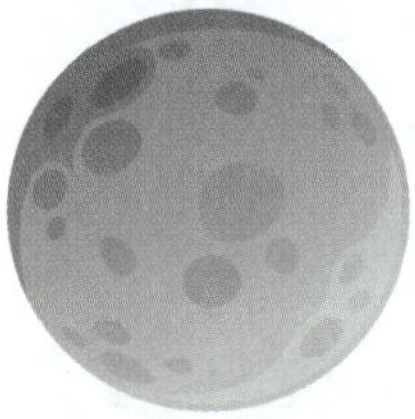

7 Owl ☐

8 Bee ☐

9 Cloud ☐

10 Pigeon ☐

Literacy Skills

19 Computer Keyboard

On a computer keyboard, there are letter keys, number keys, symbol keys, action keys and some buttons. Each of them perform a different function.

Read each line and tick (✓) the correct key.

1 Move down

a 

b 

2 Mute volume

a 

b 

3 Go to the next line

a 

b 

4 Space bar

a 

b 

5 Switch off

a 

b 

Whiz fact

Most computer keyboards are called QWERTY keyboards because their first six letters from the top left are Q, W, E, R, T, Y!

20 COVID Hygiene

We must all do or not do some things to stay safe from COVID-19. See the pictures and make a  *for things that we must do and a*  *for things that we must not do!*

1 

Wash your hands regularly.

2 

Wear mask when you go outside to play with your friends.

3 

Touch your nose with dirty hands.

4 

Put pencil or pen in your mouth.

5 

Gather around the ice-cream shop without wearing your mask properly.

6 

Clean hands with sanitizer.

Whiz quiz

Answer these questions. The first answer has one blank. The second has two blanks, and so on...

1. Who should take care of my health? ....
2. COVID was first seen in the year 20 ....
3. Short form of work-from-home: ....
4. What we should wear when we go out: ....
5. COVID comes from a ....

Sports

21 Games We All Know

Using the words given in the help box, write the names of the games to which these terms belong.

1

Bowler

Fielder

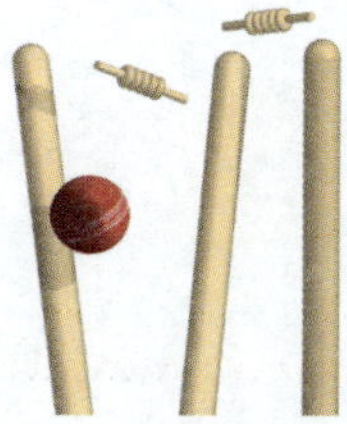
Wicket ....

2

Knight

Checkmate

Queen ....

3

Goalpost

Referee

Red card ....

4

Dribble

Lay-up

Basket ....

Help box

basketball football chess cricket

Whiz fact

India does not have an official national game. Cricket and hockey are popular games of India.

22 Taste Poem

Look at the pictures and complete this taste poem using the words given in the help box.

I like sweet things
Like ice cream and (1) ....

And pancakes with honey
And vanilla (2) ....!

I like sour things
Chaat with tamarind (3) ....

And raw mango and lime
And (4) .... with my roti.

I like salty things
Like nachos and (5) ....

Like pizza with lots of cheese
Like peanuts and (6) ....

I like spicy things
Like slices of yellow (7) ....

And chutney with lots of chillies
And freshly cracked (8) ....

I like bitter things
Like karela juice and (9) ....

And powdered brown (10) ....
They are not as bad as they seem!

Help box

neem cake chips coffee pickle
shake pepper ginger dip sauce

Whiz quiz

Name one sweet and one sour thing you like to eat.

(1) ....

(2) ....

Life Skills

23 Careful Careless

SELF AWARENESS

Draw a smiley for the good habits and a sad face for the bad habits.

1 

Exercising in the morning ☐

2 

Talking while eating ☐

3 

Biting nails ☐

4 

Washing hands before and after eating ☐

5 

Eating healthy food ☐

6 

Sneezing without covering the mouth ☐

7

Troubling animals

8

Putting finger in the ear

9

Coughing into the elbow

10

Combing hair neatly

11

Walking carefully around puddles

12

Watching cartoons on phone in the night

Whiz fact

Being clean and tidy is a part of good hygiene. It helps us stay healthy and fit.

Learning Skills

24 One, Two, Three-Four-Five!

CRITICAL THINKING

Read this number rhyme.

One, two, three, four, five
Once I caught a fish alive
Six, seven, eight, nine, ten
Then I let it go again.
Why did you let it go?
Because it bit my finger so!
Which finger did it bite?
This little finger on the right.

Count the underlined objects and write 1, 2, 3, 4 or 5 in the boxes.

1. 

   How many suns are there in the sky? ☐

2. 

   How many wheels are there in a tricycle? ☐

3. 

   How many fingers are there in one hand? ☐

4. 

   How many wings does a bird have? ☐

5

How many babies are there in a pair of twins?

6

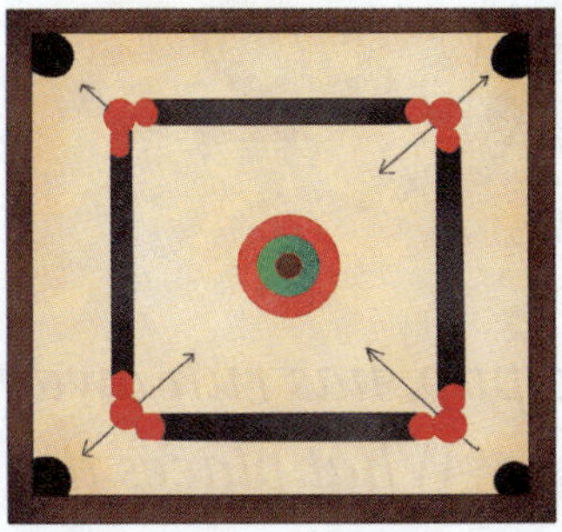

How many pockets does a carrom board have?

7

How many suits are there in a pack of cards?

8

How many school days are there in a week?

9

How many tails does a dog have?

10

How many colours are there in a traffic light?

Whiz fact

The words duo, duet, pair and couple all mean a set of two.

25 Places Near Us

Lola the pup, has run away from home. She has been to many places near her house. What places did Lola visit? Write the names with words from the help box.

Help box

school park bookstore post office

cinema restaurant vegetable stall

Whiz fact

Places around our house form our neighbourhood. It is always safe to go around the neighbourhood with a parent, elder sister, elder brother or a family member we trust.

India Focus

26 We Celebrate

Look at the pictures of some festivals of India and write their names using the words given in the help box.

1 .... is the festival of lights.

2 .... is the festival of colours.

Help box

Christmas | Holi | Eid-ul-Fitr | Diwali | Gurpurab

Whiz fact

A day on which we remember someone great is called a *jayanti* in India. Gandhi Jayanti is an example of such a day.

3 .... is a festival celebrated at the end of the holy month of Ramadan.

4 .... is a festival celebrated on 25 December every year.

5 .... is a festival to celebrate the birthday of Guru Nanak.

Whiz quiz

Write the names of two *jayantis*.

1 ....

2 ....

27 Rhyme Time

Look at the pictures and complete the rhymes with the help of the words given in the help box.

I am a Little Teapot

I am a little (1) ....
Short and stout
This is my (2) ....
This is my (3) ....
When the (4) .... is boiling

Hear me shout
"Just pick me up
and pour me out!"

Help box

water teapot handle spout

Incy Wincy Spider

Incy Wincy spider
Went up the water
1 .... ,
Down came the
2 ....
And washed the
spider out.

Incy Wincy spider
Went up the water
3 .... ,
Down came the
4 ....
And washed the
spider out.

Help box

sun | spout | rain | dried

28 Our Helpers

Many people make our lives easier by helping us. Some people come to our homes in the morning to do different jobs. They are called morning callers.

Look at the pictures and write the names of these helpers using the words given in the help box.

1

A .... brings packets or bottles of milk.

2

A .... brings newspapers in the morning.

3

A .... brings fresh vegetables.

4

A .... delivers packages and letters.

Whiz fact

Scrap dealers visit our homes to buy old papers, cardboards and bottles. They sell these waste materials to shops or factories.

5

A ....
takes away trash.

6

A ....
washes the car in the morning.

7

A ....
protects us from thieves.

8

A ....
makes food for us.

Help box

vegetable seller | postman | milkman | paperboy | car washer | garbage collector | cook | police officer

Whiz quiz

What is a scrap dealer called in your language?

....

World Today

29 Mask it up!

Read the following statements and choose the correct option.

1. We should/should not wear masks when we meet people, because of COVID.

2. COVID-19 is a virus. It can/cannot go from one person to another when they breathe, talk, cough or sneeze.

3. When others wear a mask, the virus can/cannot reach you.

4. Masks will/will not block oxygen, so they are safe to wear.

5 If you are in an area where many people are infected with the coronavirus, you should/ should not wear a mask.

6 In a crowded place, even if you are outdoors, it is better to wear/to not wear a mask.

7 If you travel by a public transport, you must/must not wear a mask.

8 Cloth masks are as good as/not as good as surgical (disposable) masks. But the best germ-blockers are called 'respirators'. They have names like KN95 or KF94.

Life on Land

30 Let Us Save

Look at the pictures and fill in the blanks using the words given in the help box.

1 Use a ....  to carry things while shopping.

2 Switch off the ....  when you do not need them.

3 Close the ....  when not in use.

4 Go to a park on a ....  with your parents.

5 Wrap gifts in old .... 

.

6 Take the ....  to go up the floor.

Help box

stairs newspaper bicycle tap cloth bag lights

Whiz quiz

Find out from your parents which of these use the most electricity.

a. Light bulb b. Air-conditioner c. Fan d. Television

Life Skills

31 Safe at Home

Complete the sentences using words given in the help box.

1. If we walk with a glass full of water or milk, it can ....

2. If we open or close a door in a hurry, our finger can get ....

3. If we .... our fingers into electric sockets, we might get a shock.

4. If we open an umbrella without looking around, it can .... people in the eye.

5. If we play rough, we might .... and hurt ourselves.

Help box

poke	stick	fall	jammed	spill

Sports

32 Team or Solo

Write the names of these sports using the words given in the help box. Draw a 🙂 *if the sport is played by one person and* 🙂 🙂 *if the sport is always played in a team.*

1

....

2

....

3

....

4

....

5

6

7

8

Help box

basketball swimming hockey cricket
gymnastics chess football golf

Whiz fact

Quidditch is an imaginary sport in the *Harry Potter* books and is played by witches and wizards on broomsticks. It is now played by Muggles as well, but on the ground!

33 India in Colours

Colour the pictures of some common dishes of India as per the colour assigned to its number.

Whiz fact

The saffron flower has orange strands or threads. These give a lovely orange or yellow colour to many dishes.

34 Means of Transport

We walk or use a vehicle to go from one place to another.

Read the riddles and guess the names of the vehicles given in the help box.

I am long and winding,
my wheels move on a track.
I have wagons and an engine,
thac-thac-thac-thac-thac-thac!

1 ....

I am huge and long,
yet, I can fly.
I have wings and a tail.
See me up in the sky.

2 ....

I can be black,
or green, or even yellow.
Three wheels and a meter,
Just tell me where to go!

3 ....

I need no fuel to move.
You do not need to be wealthy,
Just sit on me and pedal,
I will keep you hale and healthy!

4 ....

I do not move on the ground,
I do not move in the air,
But when it comes to water,
You will be glad to have me there!

5 ....

I take off from planet Earth;
I soar into the blue sky;
Then I shoot off into space;
Tell me, who am I?

6 ....

Help box

autorickshaw | train | aeroplane | boat | bicycle | rocket

Whiz fact

Most vehicles move on wheels. The first wheel was made of stone and wood.

India Focus

35 Three Seasons

India has three main seasons—summer, rainy and winter.

Look at the pictures of clothes and things. Draw for summer, for rainy and for winter in the boxes given.

1

Ice cream

2

Gumboots

3

Sunglasses

5

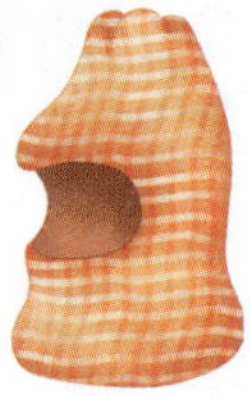

Monkey cap

4

Snowman

6

Frock

7

Sweater

Whiz fact

One of the hottest places in India is Churu in Rajasthan. It is mostly covered in sand and has very few trees. The coldest place in India is Dras in Jammu and Kashmir.

8

Gloves

9

Raincoat

10

Iced tea

11

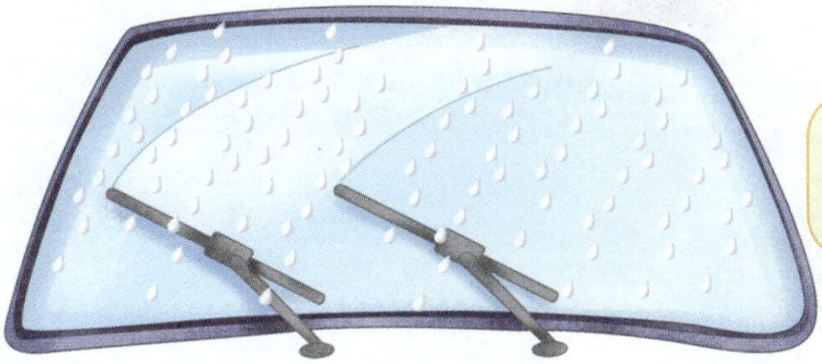

Wipers

12

Bonfire

13

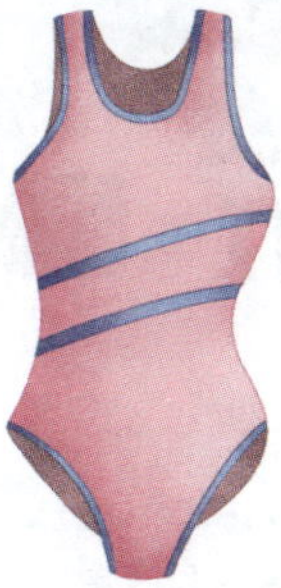

Swimsuit

14

Puddles

15

Umbrella

Learning Skills

36 Stories of Fairies

Join the pictures and letters to write the names of some fairy tales.

CRITICAL THINKING

1 Little + 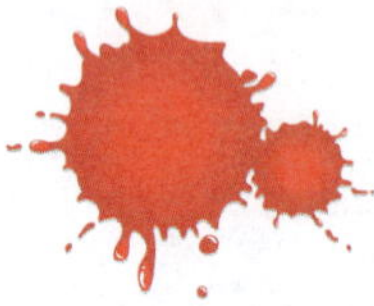 + Riding + 

2 The +  + 

3 Snow +  + and + the + 7 + 

4  + i +  + s + and + the + 3 + 

Whiz fact

Jacob and Wilhelm Grimm, known as the Brothers Grimm, were the first to write fairy tales.

India Focus

37 Indian Sweets

India is famous for its tasty sweets. Match the pictures of the sweets to their name and description.

	Sweets	Description		Pictures
1	Jalebi	Crispy curls in golden-orange sticky syrup	a	
2	Rasgulla	A white, soft and spongy sweet	b	
3	Gulab jamun	A round brown sweet in golden syrup	c	
4	Laddu	A round yellow sweet with dry fruits	d	
5	Barfi	A soft milk-based sweet with a silver coating	e	
6	Halwa	A soft and sticky sweet with dry fruits	f	

Whiz fact

Rice pudding is made of milk, rice, sugar and dry fruits. It is called *kheer* in Hindi and Marathi, *payesh* in Bengali and *payasam* in Tamil.

Language and Literature

38 The Talkative Tortoise

Read the story of the talkative tortoise. Write the correct number below each picture to match them to the correct paragraphs.

1 Long long ago near a lake with a breeze
Lived three friends: a tortoise and two geese.
They splashed about in the water so fresh.
Tortoise ate leaves, the geese had the fish.

2 One year, it didn't rain, and the lake went dry;
Everyone was so thirsty, they wanted to cry.
In the distance, from atop a tall tree,
They saw another lake, and they went, "Yippee!"

3 "There's a lovely lake in the valley there,
Lots of water and fish and leaves to spare!"
"We can fly, you know, no problem, nothing.
But what about you, you have no wings!?"

4 Tortoise replied, "Clamp this stick in your beaks,
I'll hold on." The geese said, "Just don't speak!"
And they took off: The geese and the tortoise
Held on to the stick, And they flew and flew.

5 The village kids saw the three friends.
They exclaimed, "Oh look! Look at them!"
The tortoise was thrilled to see the kids cheer,
He smiled and said, "Thanks, my dears!"

6 Alas, the moment he made that sound,
The silly tortoise fell and hit the ground.
The geese could do nothing about their friend,
He didn't listen, and so he met his end.

39 Useful Plants

Plants and trees are very useful to us.

Read the lines about some plants and trees and fill in the blanks using the words given in the help box.

1. A rose bush has sharp thorns but it gives us sweet-smelling ....

2. A mango tree has lovely green leaves and yummy ....

3. A banyan tree has lots of branches and leaves that gives us ....

4 A capsicum plant gives us red, green or yellow

....

5 A cotton plant has many white buds. We spin them into

....

6 A sunflower plant has big and bright yellow flowers. We get .... from it.

Help box

oil flowers cloth fruits shade vegetables

Whiz fact

An indigo plant has blue-purple flowers which are used to make a bluish colour called indigo.

India Focus

40 National Symbols of India

Fill in the blanks using the words given in the help box.

Tricolour

1 The national .... has saffron, white and green stripes. It has a navy blue wheel at the centre.

Tiger

2 The national .... is found in forests. It has yellow and black stripes.

Peacock

3 The national .... has many colours. Its neck is a beautiful blue. It has long feathers that open like a fan.

Whiz fact

The national emblem of India has four lions standing on a band with a wheel at the centre. Below the wheel are the words *Satyameva Jayate*, which mean 'Truth Alone Triumphs'.

4 The national .... is yummy, juicy and golden-yellow. We eat it a lot in summers.

Mango

Lotus

5 The national .... is pink or white. It has big and round leaves.

Banyan

6 The national .... is huge and shady. It has many long, thick and hanging roots.

Help box

animal tree fruit
flower flag bird

Whiz quiz

We all have seen the National Emblem of India. Can you tell where?

Responsible Consumptions & Production

41 Swish Party

A swish party is a party in which you can swap your clothes, toys, books or other things with your friends. Each child gets some new things, gives away some old things, and there is no wastage!

These children have attended a swish party, and have exchanged their things with their friends. Follow the arrows and draw along the strings to see who has got what. Then fill in the blanks in the lines on this page.

1. Abeer has gifted his ……………………………… to ……………………………… .

2. Chaitali has gifted her ……………………………… to Harsh.

3. Esha has gifted her ……………………………… to Jayanti.

4. ……………………………… has gifted his ……………………………… to Lakshya.

5. Ira has gifted her ……………………………… books to Falguni.

6. ……………………………… has gifted his blanket to ……………………………… .

Whiz fact

Make sure that if you organise a swish, you only swap things that are in good condition, with no tears, breakages or missing parts. You wouldn't want to get damaged or badly kept things, would you?

Abeer
tennis racquet
Bani
Chaitali
red sweater
Dhruv
Esha
skates
Falguni
Girish
HARRY POTTER
Harry Potter books
Harsh
Ira
scrunchies
Jayanti
Karam
blanket
Lakshya

Literacy Skills

42 Emoji Fun

TECHNOLOGY

Emojis are small pictures of faces, animals, people, common things and places. They are used to add feelings to messages sent through phones or computers.

Tick the correct emojis to match with the feelings.

1 Happy — a ☐   b ☐

2 Sleepy — a ☐   b ☐

3 Surprised — a ☐   b ☐

4 Bored — a ☐   b ☐

5 Confused — a ☐   b ☐

6 Sad — a ☐   b ☐

Whiz fact

Emoji is a Japanese word. 'E' means picture and 'moji' means character.

43 Hidden Animals

Find the animals hidden in this jungle and have fun colouring them.

Learning Skills

44 Monster Shadows

Tick (✓) the correct pictures to match the shadows to the monsters.

CRITICAL THINKING

1

a

b

2

a

b

3

a

b

4

a

b

Literacy Skills

45 Spot it!

DATA HANDLING

Look at this picture and read the lines about things in the picture. Write the correct number in the circles.

1 A small red insect with black spots 

2 A snake in the bushes 

3 A pink flower with a yellow heart 

4 A round white pebble 

5 A bird on a branch 

6 A leaf in the pond 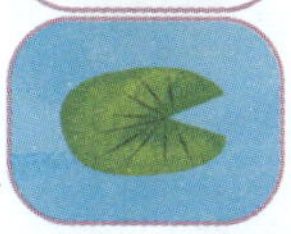

46 Missing Pieces

Some pieces of this picture are missing. Each missing piece has been replaced with a shape.

Draw the shapes in the boxes to find the right place of each missing piece.

1

2

3

4

Quiz Yourself 1

Choose the correct options to fill in the blanks.

1 We have .... fingers in both hands.

(a) one (b) six (c) two (d) ten

2 A big .... with the name of our school on it takes us to school.

(a) bus (b) car (c) cab (d) bug

3 A dog or a cat that lives at home is a ....

(a) bet (b) set (c) pet (d) net

4 An apple and a lychee are .... in colour.

(a) green (b) red (c) yellow (d) blue

5 A .... eats cheese.

(a) bat (b) cat (c) rat (d) mat

6 We can eat chips and nachos with a ....

(a) dip (b) lip (c) sip (d) tip

7 A .... is a bird.

(a) pen (b) den (c) yen (d) hen

8 If we play with sharp scissors, we might .... ourselves.

(a) bite (b) cut (c) pain (d) hit

9 The water is boiling, so the .... is almost ready!

(a) sea (b) pot (c) ice (d) tea

10 The best respirators are called ....

(a) K95 (b) N99 (c) X55 (d) F25

Quiz Yourself 2

Choose the correct options to fill in the blanks.

1 1 We get .... from sunflowers.

(a) tea (b) lot (c) oil (d) soy

2 Aeroplanes and rockets fly in the ....

(a) sky (b) shy (c) spy (d) sly

3 Turn off the .... to save water.

(a) cap (b) map (c) zap (d) tap

4 The peacock has long feathers that open like a ....

(a) fan (b) cap (c) tap (d) can

5 Eid-ul-Fitr is a festival celebrated at the .... of Ramzan.

(a) all (b) end (c) dot (d) hot

6 :) means happy, :(means ....

(a) joy (b) ill (c) sad (d) mad

7 In summer we can eat yummy .... cream.

(a) ear (b) dog (c) jam (d) ice

8 An .... is a bird we can see in the night sky.

(a) owl (b) ape (c) asp (d) emu

9 The .... shines in the day, the moon shines at night.

(a) bun (b) dun (c) sun (d) fun

10 Scooby Doo is a ....

(a) hog (b) dog (c) log (d) fog

Quiz Yourself 3

Choose the correct options to fill in the blanks.

1. We wear a hanky on our shirt using a safety ....

   (a) kit (b) pin (c) pen (d) bug

2. Brass bowl and plates, online invitation and .... are good for planet Earth.

   (a) Styrofoam (b) Wrapping paper
   (c) Plastic plates (d) Cloth buntings

3. When we come home from playing, we wipe our shoes on the ....

   (a) cat (b) mat (c) rat (d) fat

4. A big animal with horns that gives us milk is a ....

   (a) sow (b) now (c) cow (d) bow

5. We have one .... on each side of our face. We use them to hear things.

   (a) ear (b) rib (c) toe (d) eye

6. We draw lines with a sketch ....

   (a) pin (b) pan (c) pun (d) pen

7. Buzz Lightyear is a .... His friend is Woody.

   (a) soy (b) coy (c) toy (d) joy

8. I sit on a chair but sleep on a ....

   (a) pin (b) bed (c) log (d) bag

9. A bird has .... wings.

   (a) one (b) ten (c) six (d) two

10. Almonds, cashews and raisins are .... fruits.

    (a) dry (b) fry (c) cry (d) pry

Quiz Yourself 4

Choose the correct options to fill in the blanks.

1. Each morning, I drink milk out of a ....

   (a) bug (b) mug (c) rug (d) pug

2. I keep my little things in a round ....

   (a) fin (b) pin (c) yin (d) tin

3. If it meows, it is a ....

   (a) dog (b) cat (c) bus (d) rat

4. We play cricket with a .... and a ball.

   (a) nut (b) hat (c) bat (d) fan

5. A hen lays an ...., which becomes a chick.

   (a) oil (b) owl (c) imp (d) egg

6. The longest key on a keyboard is the space ....

   (a) bar (b) car (c) jar (d) tar

7. Use a cloth .... to carry things while shopping.

   (a) tag (b) rag (c) gag (d) bag

8. The power button is used to switch the computer on and ....

   (a) all (b) off (c) use (d) ink

9. An .... is a small insect with six thin legs.

   (a) elk (b) owl (c) ant (d) eel

10. When we order food from a restaurant, it usually comes in a ....

    (a) box (b) fox (c) nox (d) pox

Answer Key

Page 9: 1. cheeks; 2. chin; 3. lips; 4. Teeth; 5. hair; 6. Eyes; 7. ears; 8. nose; 9. fingers; 10. toes; 11. Hands

Page 10-11: 1. ✓; 2. ✓; 3. ✗; 4. ✓; 5. ✗; 6. ✓; 7. ✓; 8. ✗; 9. ✓; 10. ✗; 11. ✗; 12. ✗

Page 14: 1. cat-mat; 2. dog-log; 3. pin-tin; 4. jug-mug; 5. bake-cake; 6. mouse-house

Page 15: 1. red; 2. pink; 3. orange; 4. green; 5. purple; 6. yellow

Page 16: 1. B; 2. A; 3. B; 4. A; 5. A; 6. B; 7. B

Page 17: 1. ✓; 2. ✓; 3. ✗; 4. ✗; 5. ✓; 6. ✓; 7. ✓; 8. ✗; 9. ✓

Page 18: 2. b, c; 3. a, c; 4. a, b; 5. b, c

Page 19: 1. ☺; 2. ☹; 3. ☺; 4. ☺; 5. ☺; 6. ☹; 7. ☹; 8. ☺; 9 ☹

Page 20: 1. ✓; 2. ✗; 3. ✓; 4. ✗; 5. ✓

Page 21: 1. Soft; 2. Sticky; 3. Hard; 4. Spongy; 5. Rough; 6. Pointy

Page 22: 1. e; 2. d; 3. a; 4. b; 5. c

Page 23: 1. mouse; 2. dog; 3. man; 4. bear; 5. lion; 6. girl

Page 24-25: Kitchen: 2, 6, 8, 11; **Bathroom:** 1, 10, 14; **Bedroom:** 3, 4, 12, 15; **Living room:** 5, 9, 13; **Garage:** 7

Page 26-27: 1. W; 2. D; 3. W; 4. W; 5. D; 6. W; 7. W; 8. D; 9. W; 10. D; 11. W; 12. D

Page 28: 1. ay, ep; 2. tri, si; 3. bu, sl

Page 29: A. 2, 1, 3; B. 3, 2, 1; C. 1, 3, 2; D. 2, 1, 3

Page 30: 1. D; 2. N; 3. D; 4. N; 5. D; 6. N; 7. N; 8. D; 9. D; 10. D

Page 31: 1. b; 2. a; 3. b; 4. b; 5. a

Page 32: 1. ☺; 2. ☺; 3. ☹; 4. ☹; 5. ☹; 6. ☺

Page 33: 1. cricket; 2. chess; 3. football; 4. basketball

Page 34-35: 1. cake; 2. shake; 3. sauce; 4. pickle; 5. dip; 6. chips; 7. ginger; 8. pepper; 9. neem; 10. coffee

Page 36-37: 1. ☺; 2. ☹; 3. ☹; 4. ☺; 5. ☺; 6. ☹; 7. ☹; 8. ☹; 9. ☺; 10. ☺; 11. ☺; 12. ☹

Page 38-39: 1. 1; 2. 3; 3. 5; 4. 2; 5. 2; 6. 4; 7. 4; 8. 5; 9. 1; 10. 3

Page 40-41: 1. cinema; 2. restaurant; 3. school; 4. post office; 5. vegetable stall; 6. bookstore; 7. park

Page 42-43: 1. Diwali; 2. Holi; 3. Eid-ul-Fitr; 4. Christmas; 5. Gurpurab

Page 44-45: I am a Little Teapot
1. teapot; 2. handle; 3. spout; 4. water

Incy Wincy Spider 1. spout; 2. rain; 3. sun; 4. dried

Page 46-47: 1. milkman; 2. paperboy; 3. vegetable seller; 4. postman; 5. garbage collector; 6. car washer; 7. police officer; 8. cook

Page 48-49: 1. should; 2. can; 3. cannot; 4. will not; 5. should; 6. to wear; 7. must; 8. as good as

Page 50: 1. cloth bag; 2. lights; 3. tap; 4. bicycle; 5. newspaper; 6. stairs

Page 51: 1. spill; 2. jammed; 3. stick; 4. poke; 5. fall

Page 52-53: 1. cricket ☺☺; 2. golf ☺ ; 3. basketball ☺☺ ; 4. football ☺☺ ; 5. swimming ☺ ; 6. gymnastics ☺; 7. chess ☺ ; 8. hockey ☺☺

Page 56-57: 1. train; 2. aeroplane; 3. autorickshaw; 4. bicycle; 5. boat; 6. rocket

Page 58-59: 1. ☼; 2. 🌧; 3. ☼; 4. 🌲 5. 🌲; 6. ☼; 7. 🌲; 8. 🌲; 9. 🌧; 10. ☼ 11. 🌧; 12. 🌲; 13. ☼; 14. 🌧; 15. 🌧

Page 60: 1. Little Red Riding Hood; 2. The Frog Prince; 3. Snow White and the 7 Dwarfs; 4. Goldilocks and the 3 Bears

Page 61: 1. f; 2. d; 3. a; 4. e; 5. b; 6. c

Page 62-63: 4, 2, 5, 1, 6, 3

Page 64-65: 1. flowers; 2. fruits; 3. shade; 4. vegetables; 5. cloth; 6. oil

Page 66-67: 1. flag; 2. animal; 3. bird; 4. fruit; 5. flower; 6. tree

Page 68-69: 1. red sweater, Bani; 2. skates; 3. scrunchies; 4. Girish, tennis racquet; 5. Harry Potter books; 6. Karam, Dhruv

Page 70: 1. a; 2. b; 3. b; 4. a; 5. a; 6. b

Page 72: 1. a; 2. b; 3. a; 4. b

Page 73:

Page 74: 1. ; 2. ; 3. ; 4. 

Page 75: Quiz Yourself 1: 1. d; 2. a; 3. c; 4. b; 5. c; 6. a; 7. d; 8. b; 9. d; 10. a

Page 76: Quiz Yourself 2: 1. c; 2. a; 3. d; 4. a; 5. b; 6. c; 7. d; 8. a; 9. c; 10. b

Page 77: Quiz Yourself 3: 1. b; 2. d; 3. b; 4. c; 5. a; 6. d; 7. c; 8. b; 9. d; 10. a

Page 78: Quiz Yourself 4: 1. b; 2. d; 3. b; 4. c; 5. d; 6. a; 7. d; 8. b; 9. c; 10. a